# COMFORT

## *in Time of*

# BEREAVEMENT

Scriptures and Inspirational Support
During the Time of the Death of a
Loved One

## GEROME SINGLETERRY

ISBN 978-1-0980-2877-0 (paperback)
ISBN 978-1-0980-2879-4 (digital)

Christian Faith Publishing, Inc.
832 Park Avenue
Meadville, PA 16335
www.christianfaithpublishing.com

Printed in the United States of America

# THANKS BE TO GOD

I would like to thank God, for giving me the knowledge, the patience, and the wisdom to write this book. He deserves all the credit because I only write what he tells me to.

# CONTENTS

# PREFACE

Bereavement is one of the toughest things we will have to face in our lives, but with the help of God we will be able to get through it. I really hope this book will help those who read it, find peace and understanding when they have a love one to die, or a love one that has already died. All ways remember, God is in control of any situation you might be facing.

# CHAPTER 1

# **Death**

**Webster's definition of death—act
of dying, state of being dead**

Death is not welcomed by no one including Christians, but we all have to die.
Hebrews 9:27 says, "And it is appointed unto
men once to die, but after this the judgment."
God never intended for us to die, but there
is no way to escape it, unless he comes back
while you are alive. God is immortal and will
never die, and when he created us in his image,
that's what he intended for us. Death became
a part of man when Adam and Eve disobeyed
God in the Garden of Eden and listened to
Satan instead. That was the biggest mistake

they made, and the human race started dying at that very moment.

> And t he serpent said unto the woman, ye shall not surely die. (Gen. 3:4)

I know you probably have heard on the news or in a courtroom—the court sentenced someone to death. This is what the judge says to the prisoner when he renders a death verdict. We all received a death penalty from God because of the disobedience of Adam and Eve. Just thinking about death can bring fear and sadness to your heart, and when this happens, you can become a slave to it. Most people don't like discussing burial insurance or funeral plans because they fear death. They would rather not talk about it, thinking it will go away. Death is something appointed to all of us by God. We all have to do it before we reach our final destination.

> O death, where is thy sting? O grave, Where is thy victory? (2 Cor. 15:55)

We should all be happy when that day comes because if we are saved, we will leave out our sinful body, take on our glorified body in Christ, and live with him in heaven for eternity. What could be better than that? Nonbelievers don't think like this, they think of death ass the end and there is no life after it. Jesus showed us by him dying on the cross and being raised from the grave that's not true. Death is an enemy of God, and Satan uses it to keep us in bondage to him. You can be free of this fear of death and bondage if you trust in God.

> For we which live are always delivered unto death for Jesus sake, that the life also of Jesus might be made manifest in our mortal flesh. (2 Cor. 4:11)

We received life from God the day we were born, and only he can control it and our destiny. We also start dying that same day because of sin. The body has to die, but the soul never will. This makes all of us immortal whether you believe in God or not. This is what he gave

man when he created him. You can ask anyone you see this question, "Do you want to
die?" Most of the people will say no, including
Christians. Everyone is afraid of the unknown,
but with Jesus, we don't have to be afraid; he
experienced death and came back from it.

> But we see Jesus, who was
> made a little lower than angels
> for the suffering of death,
> crowned with glory and
> honor, that he by the grace
> of God should taste death for
> every man. (Heb. 2:9)

Living in sin separates us from the power
of God, and when we do this, we become
afraid of death. If you live your life in Jesus,
you will never have to fear it because he has
already overcome death.

> For the wages of sin is death;
> but the gift of God is eternal
> life through Jesus Christ our
> Lord. (Rom. 6:23)

Death has its place in this world, but it will never have victory over those who follow Jesus and trust in him. We can have peace when we face it because God will give us the strength to do it. Yes, we all will see some of our friends and family die before us, but we have faith in God we will see them again.

> Yea though I walk through the valley of the shadow of death, I will fear no evil: for thou art with me; thy rod and thy staff they comfort me. (Ps. 23:4)

Only God can comfort you in any situation you are facing even in the time of your own death. Discussing death is not a popular conversation and many people try to avoid it. This is a conversation we should have without having any fear at all; it is just a part of life. God is above death, and it has no power over him and those who believe in him have that same power. Jesus is alive and well and sitting at the right hand of his father in heaven, and those who believe in him, when they die, will be with them.

> And God shall wipe away all tears from their eyes; and there shall be no more death, neither sorrow, nor crying, neither shall there be any more pain: for the former things are passed away. (Rev. 21:4)

Just think about this for a moment, a time will come where there will be no more death and pain. Death will cease to exist because it was never meant to be a part of man's life. When this happens, it will be a beautiful time, and no one will ever die again. God created us to live for eternity and not to die, that's why he gave us a part of his soul—when he breaths the breath of life into Adam.

> I am he that liveth, and was dead; and, behold, I am alive for evermore, Amen; and have the keys of hell and of death. (Rev. 1:8)

In the life to come, there will be no more death. God has a beautiful ending to it. He gives us eternal life with him in heaven. Thank God we don't have to be sad when some of our love one die because death has already been defeated. Satan cannot give life he can only try to steal it. If he had his way, our souls would never live again they would just remain in the grave.

> But God will redeem my soul
> from the power of the grave:
> for he shall receive me. Selah.
> (Ps. 49:15)

Can you imagine a place where people will never get sick, have no pains, and never die? That place is heaven. There will be no need for hospitals, doctors, nurses, or morticians' there. The body will never grow old and be weak again, and no one there will know what death is. The funeral homes represent death, but the good news is, God is life. As long as we have accepted Jesus as our

Lord and savior and walk with him, we will have eternal life.

> For whoso findeth me findeth life, and shall obtain favor of the Lord. (Prov. 8:35)

As long as you live in this world, death will always be an evil presence because Satan is the force behind it. Have you ever witnessed a flower when it starts to bloom during spring it is so beautiful and full of life, but when winter comes, it becomes withered, ugly, and has no life. Death is like winter, it always brings ugliness and never brings life. God is like spring, he always brings beauty and life. We can rejoice because we have God with us during our time of sadness.

> Jesus saith unto him, I am the way, the truth, and the life: no man cometh unto the Father but by me. (John 14:6)

When death happens in a family, it can affect them in so many ways—financially, mentally, and spiritually. Some people blame God for their lost, and some even blame themselves and other family members. This is just a deception of Satan of how he uses death to keep us afraid and confused. Death can be devastating, but we don't have to let it devastate us when one of our love ones dies. We have God by our side. He is bigger than death and always will be.

> For me to live is Christ, and
> to die is gain. (Phil. 1:21)

Most people would think that you are crazy if you told them you will gain eternal life when you die. Everyone will have eternal life when they die, but the question is, where they will spend it? Some people will spend their life in heaven, and unfortunately some will spend there's in hell. Death can't follow you to heaven, but it certainly will follow you to hell. God has shown man that all life is in him, and Satan has no power over it.

The final judgment of death will be done by God when he judges everyone for their sins.

> So then every one of us shall give an account of himself to God. (Rom. 14:12)

# CHAPTER 2

# The Loss of a Loved One

**Webster's definition of loss—act or
instance of loosing, something lost**

Everyone has lost someone that is close to them to death. It could have been a family member or a close friend. When this happens, you feel a loss and emptiness. Someone you love and really care about has been taken away from you. You start to feel all alone, and your heart is sadly broken. Sometimes, you just want to give up and stop living yourself. There are not enough tears to express how you feel at that moment. Memories of the good times with then seem to never stop filling your mind. Those memories are the spirit of God, letting you know that everything is going to be all right. No one will expect you to get over your loss quickly, but with the love of God in your heart, it will be easier.

You will never forget about them, but God will help you to go on with your life. If you allow him to help you, in time, it will become easier, and you will understand that your love one is not lost they are just in a better place. Along the way, it will be hard at first, but God will be there to support you every step of the way. You are the one experiencing this loss and have to deal with it. I know it's easier said than done, but remember, you are not alone. With God, you can get through anything no matter how tough it is.

> But Jesus beheld them, and said unto them, with men this is impossible; but with God all things are possible. (Matt. 19:26)

What God wants us to understand is not to rely on man to solve our problems because he can't. It's not wrong to confide in someone you trust when you are feeling sad, but don't never forget about God. He has all of the right answers to give you for the pain you are feeling. The reason a lot people hurt for such a long period of time after the loss of a love one is they forget about God and never seek him for comfort. He can't help you unless you call on him. Sometimes, there might be no one for you to talk to, but God will always be there.

It might seem to you that you will never get over this, but God has a plan to show you that you can. There is nothing impossible to him, and all power is in his hands. God created everything that is good, and he will be your comforter during your time of sorrow. He will also be your strength to get you through this. He does this because he loves you and understands how you feel, and he wants to comfort you. Remember, if you believe in Jesus and the resurrection, your love one is not dead, they are just sleeping. I believe when someone is asleep, they are resting and at peace. This should bring you comfort knowing that your love one is resting and at peace.

Jesus said unto her; I am the resurrection, and the life: he that believeth in me, though he were dead, yet shall he live. (John 11:25)

Rest assured, on the promise of Jesus, your love one is not dead, they will live again. Jesus was crucified and buried. Everyone thought he was dead, and they would never see him again, but he rose from the grave. When he rose, he conquered death and now it has no power over us. God created us to live an eternal life and to never die, but Satan bought death upon man through Adam and Eve disobedient to God. If you can believe and trust in God, he will give you peace during your time of your loss. He knows the pain and grief that you are going through. Lean on him, and he will give you strength. I know it's hard for you to understand why God didn't heal your love one, but God never makes a mistake he has a better plan.

> For my thoughts are not your thoughts, neither are your ways my ways, saith the Lord. (Isa. 55:8)

God will never think the way we do, our way of thinking is very weak and can't compare to his. God is all powerful, and there is no weakness in him. He knows your love one is not dead, and if you would only trust him, he will show you how not to worry. When one of our love one dies, our emotions starts to take control of us, not giving us time to think about Jesus.

> For as the heavens are higher than the earth, so are my ways higher than your ways, and my thoughts than your thoughts. (Isa. 55:9)

We limit God by not believing that he can do the things he said he will do. God has all power in his hands, and he can do anything. Let him have his way in your life during this time of sorrow, and you will find rest and peace. There is no power on this earth that is higher than God's. Death will never have any power over God, and if we believe in him, it will never have any power over us.

> So when this corruptible shall have put on incorruption, and this mortal shall have put on immortality, then shall be brought to pass the saying that is written, death is swallowed up in victory. Death where is thy sting? Grave, where is thy victory? (1 Cor. 15: 54–55

If your love one repented of their sin and received Jesus as their Lord and savior, you can have comfort in knowing that they will be in heaven, and you will see them again. When we die out of this mortal body, our soul lives on and becomes immortal. Death and the grave have no hold on us, and we don't have to be afraid of that anymore. Your love one just made that transition that we all will have to make one day, just keep God in your heart.

> And as it is appointed unto
> men once to die, but after
> this the judgment. (Heb.
> 9:27)

No one will escape death unless Jesus returns before you die. The loss of your love one hurts deeply, but God will show you how to get through it because death is not final.

> We know that we have passed
> from death unto life, because
> we love the brethren. He that
> loveth not his brother abi-
> deth in death. (1 John 3:14)

The love and the forgiveness that God gives us is the power to overcome death. Only those who haven't accepted Jesus will be defeated by it. It hurts now, and you feel like you will never get over this loss, but in time, you will. God created us for his purpose, and one of those purposes is to live with him in heaven for eternity. When sin entered into the world through Adam and Eve, the human body started to die. Death is an enemy, and

Satan uses it as one of his weapons to make us afraid. If you are familiar with the story in the Bible about the little girl that died, her parents and the rulers of the synagogue were afraid.

> As soon as Jesus heard the word that was spoken. He saith unto the ruler of the synagogue, be not afraid, only believe. (Mark 5:36)

Always keep your faith and trust in God, and he will help you get through anything. When tragedy is at your door, remember God is already there. It's normal to cry when one of our love one dies because that's an emotional reaction of showing your love for them. God knows you love them, and your emotional expression of that love is good for you. He also wants you to understand they are in a better place, and if you believe and trust in him, you will see them again one day. That's the comfort we all can receive from God when a love one dies.

And when he was come in,
he saith unto them, why
make ye this ado, and weep?
The damsel is not dead, but
sleepeth. (Mark 5:39)

When we lose a love one or a friend to death, it shouldn't be a sad occasion, but it always will be because we are human. God understands that part of your heart, and he knows Satan uses death as a weapon against you. But if you allow Satan to use death and fear to control you, you will never get over the death of a love one. God would never want you to live like that he loves you too much. He wants you to have peace and understanding during your time of bereavement.

Listen to God as he speaks to your heart, and he will give you all the comfort you will need. Death can never control God he controls it. He showed us that when Jesus was crucified, buried, and rose from the grave, death would never have any power over us. There is no reason to be afraid or sad; we serve a living

God. Stay in prayer with him daily during this time, and you will grow stronger.

> Jesus said unto her, I am the resurrection and the life: he that believeth in me though he were dead, yet shall he live. (John 11:25)

God is immortal and will never die, and those who believe this will become like him. You can find comfort in knowing that your love one does have a soul and will live again.

> And whosoever liveth and believeth in me shall never die, believest thou this? (John 11: 26)

I don't know what you believe in or trust, but I believe every word of that to be true. God couldn't make it any clearer than this, if we believe in him we will never die. The pain and suffering you are going through want last, because God will see you through it. Your love one is in a better place, and when you start to believe it you will have peace. They are not lost and never will be. Remember death is not the final chapter it's the beginning of a new one.

> Wherefore he saith, awake thou that sleepest. And arise from the dead, and Christ shall give the light. (Eph. 5:14)

We will all hear the trumpet sound and the voice of God calling us up from the grave to face judgment. Until then the Holy Spirit will be your comforter to see you through this.

> I have been young and now am old; yet have I not seen the righteous forsaken, nor his seed begging bread. (Ps. 36:25)

# CHAPTER 3

# Grief

## Webster's definition of grief— great unhappiness, win, failure

Now that your love one has died, you will be facing grief and pain every day, making it very difficult to live a normal life. One thing that can make anyone very unhappy and sad is when someone they love dies. God never intended for death to be a part of man's life because he knew it would bring grief and unhappiness to him. There have been documented stories of how one spouse dies before the other, and then the other spouse becomes so unhappy that they grieve themselves to death. That's true love. They allowed the grief of their love one to overcome them with death.

> For my life is spent with grief, and my years with sighing: my strength faileth because of mine iniquity and bones are consumed. (Ps. 31:10)

Grief will kill you if you allow it to, but with the love of God, he will show you happiness and peace during this time. Most people don't want to trust God with their emotions because they believe they can handle it on their own. We are weak, but God is strong, and we can rely on him in our times of trouble, and he will never let us down. Trust God with all of your emotions during your time of lost, and he will give you an understanding heart. Never try to handle emotional situations by yourself because you will never understand them. God will be your shoulder to cry on, and talk to.

> Peace I leave with you, my peace I give unto you: not as the world giveth, give I unto you. Let not your heart be troubled, neither let it be afraid. (John 14:27)

In order to get through your grieving and be able to function, you will need the peace of God in your heart. Allow God to come in and help you at this moment. He loves you and will never forsake or leave you alone during this time.

> And the peace of God, which passeth all understanding, shall keep your heart and minds through Christ Jesus. (Phil. 4:7)

After a love one dies, most people start grieving for a long period of time, but God don't want us to do that. He wants us to move on with our lives believing and trusting him, knowing that everything will be all right. We need to allow God to show us why things happen in our lives that we have no control over. When you do this, you will begin to understand why your love one died.

> Trust in the Lord with all thine heart: and lean not unto thine own understanding. In all thy ways acknowledges him, and he shall direct your path. (Prov. 3:5–6)

Trust is a good thing because when you do it, you are showing someone you believe in them. The more you trust God with your situation, the more he will be able to help you, and you will grow stronger. God understands your situation better than you do, and he wants to help you get through it. The peace you are looking for in your heart, he already has it for you. Allow God to work in your situation, and you truly will find understanding and peace. Unhappiness and fear don't come from God. People allow Satan to plant this seed in their heart. Depression, worry, fear, and unhappiness are spirits of

Satan, trying to deprive you of God's love and trust.

> For God hath not given us the spirit of fear; but of power, and of love, and of a sound mind. (2 Tim. 1:7)

God loves you, and he knows what you are going through and what you need. I know it's hard not to grieve when your love one dies, but too much grieving can hurt you and keep you in fear. There have been stories reported of how some people could never function normal after the death of a love one. Some even committed suicide. You need to trust God, move on with your life, and understand that death is not the end. The longer you let grief remain in your heart, the harder it will be for you to stop grieving for your love one.

> And grieve not the holy spirit of God, whereby you are sealed unto the day of redemption. (Eph. 4:30)

God is your restorer and redeemer when you are hurting and unhappy he is not pleased. What do you think heaven is like a place of sadness and unhappiness or a place full of joy and happiness? Well, that's where God lives. He wants you to be full of joy and happiness every day. There is no sadness and unhappiness in him. Keep yourself busy every day in the spirit of God. This will help you take your mind off your love one. The more you focus on your love one, the more grief you will have in your heart. Christians are not defeated by death. We are conquerors in Christ and over comers through his blood.

> Nay, in all these things we are more than conquerors through him that love us. (Rom. 8:37)

When we live in the presence of God, we have the assurance that Satan is defeated, and we don't have to fear him. God is always in control no matter how big the problem may seem. If you keep him in your heart, you will overcome it. Just try to control the feelings you are having for your love one, and allow the Holy Spirit to speak to your heart. You will soon start to feel your grief leaving you. Pray to God every day and ask him to strengthen you when you are feeling depressed and unhappy, and he will answer you.

> Blessed are they that mourn:
> for they shall be comforted.
> (Matt. 5:4)

Any time you start to feel grief, ask God to comfort you, that's the spirit of Satan trying to attack you. His spirit will always try to convince you to be sad and depressed, and there is no hope. But the Holy Spirit will always be there to let you know that Satan is a liar. Always guard your heart. God created you and your love one, and he will never do anything to hurt you or them. Your grief is only a temporary thing, and with God's love, you will soon get through it. You need him every day even when you don't have a problem, he is the one that can give you comfort in times of trouble.

> And the peace of God, which
> passeth all understanding,
> shall keep your hearts and
> minds through Christ Jesus.
> (Phil. 4:7)

Grief, pain, and suffering shouldn't have a hold on us during the time of the death of a love, but sometimes, we allow it to. Satan is always trying to plant seeds of doubt in your heart because he knows God has given those who believe in him the victory over death and the grave. You will only find peace and life in Jesus not death. Satan uses death as a weapon to keep us afraid and in bondage to him.

> It is a faithful saying: for if we
> be dead with him, we shall
> also live with him. (2 Tim.
> 2:11)

God hasn't forsaken your love one, and he hasn't forgotten your pain and the grief you are going through. Just take time to whisper to him how much you need him to help you get through this, and he will surely answer you.

Your grief and pain will soon leave because God will overshadow it with his love and understanding. God knows what grief is, he watched his only son die on a cross to save us from sin. We must all die to get out of our sinful body to receive a glorified body that God will give us and will last for eternity.

> He is despised and rejected of men; a man of sorrows and acquainted with grief: and we hid as it were our faces from him; he was despised, and we esteemed him not. (Isa. 53:3)

You don't have to have a love one die before grief can control your life. How many people you know that are unhappy and think they are failures? Grief can raise its ugly head anywhere in our lives if we allow it to.

> Cast thy burdens upon the Lord, and he shall sustain thee: he shall never suffer the righteous to be moved. (Ps. 55:22)

God is always watching over his children because he loves and cares for them so much. It really means something to become a child of God and become a member of his family. There is comfort in knowing that God cares for you the same way he cares for his son Jesus. Trust God with all your heart, and he will give you all the peace you need.

> Love not the world, neither the things that are in the world. If any man loves the world, the love of the father is not in him. (1 John 2:15)

Don't let your grief pull you down because death has no victory over your love one's or you. Jesus has already conquered death, and they will surely live again.

# CHAPTER 4

# Remembrance

**Webster's definition of
remembrance—recall to mind, not
forget, carry greetings from**

I mmediately after the death of a love one,
the good times you had with them seem to
creep into your mind, and you start to remember some of those times. Many of them are
good and some of them are bad, but your love
for them helps you to remember them both.
Some people would only choose to remember
the good times, but some of our love ones have
a bad side that we don't want to remember and
we choose not to. During the funeral, they
always have an open floor for people to speak

about the deceased. Most of those conversations are funny, and it brings back memories to all who knew them. I think remembering your love one is a good thing because it can bring healing to your broken heart.

> I thank God whom I serve from my forefathers with pure conscience, that without ceasing I have remembrance of thee in my prayers night and day. (2nd Tim. 1:3)

I can remember when my mother died, I held her hands the day before—now that's a sad moment to remember. But I choose to remember that because that was a quiet moment, and I really enjoyed doing that with her. When you are alone, that's when you start to realize that your love one is no longer with you—the remembrance of them really start to set in. You start thinking about the last thing you done with them or what you said to them before they died. Those are some of the hardest moments and very difficult to get through. But always remember you won't have to go through them alone, you will always have your family and God to help you get through it.

> Greatly desiring to see thee, being mindful of thy tears, that I might be filled with joy. (2 Tim. 1:4)

Some of the things you did with your love one, even the ones that annoyed you, can bring you happiness when you remember them. Those times can also make you sad because you know that you will no longer be able to do them anymore. Remembering your love can be a good thing, but don't let it make you sad. God wants us to be happy not sad. Remember, your love one is in a better place—actually better places than you are because they don't have to contend with this sinful world anymore.

> For his anger endureth but a moment: in his favor is life: weeping may endure for a night, but joy cometh in the morning. (Ps. 30:5)

God will not allow Satan to plant seeds of unhappiness in your heart. He will always be there with his spirit of joy and happiness to help you overcome those moments. I can also remember when my dad died. I walked into his bedroom where he laid an immediately felt his presence, speaking to me from the ceiling. He told me not to worry and that he was okay. Now that made me feel better, and I still remember that moment today. Remembering the good things about your love one can bring you happiness and peace. I think not remembering them can prolong your pain, sorrow, and can show that you really didn't care much about them.

> And he took bread and gave thanks, and brake it and gave unto them saying, this is my body which is given for you: this do in remembrance of me. (Luke 22:19)

When Jesus broke the bread of life and gave it to his disciples, he wanted them to remember him and what he was about to face. Knowing that he would be crucified and would be resurrected from the grave, he wanted them to remember what he said and those who believe in him would never die. Now, this had to be a difficult time for Jesus and his disciples, but remembering something good would bring them comfort, peace, healing, and understanding during their most difficult times. God knows how to comfort your broken heart. Allow those memories of your love one to help heal your pain and sorrow. God will always be near, but you must call on him to help you.

> I thank God, when I serve from forefathers with pure conscience, that without ceasing I have remembrance of thee in my prayers night and day. (2 Tim. 1:3)

Remembering something is a part of our daily life. It's how we let those memories affect our lives. Good or bad, they will always be there, and you can allow them to make you sad or you can choose to let them make you happy. A lot of people only want to remember the bad things about their love ones. This is not showing them love but hatred. When you do this, you will never find peace. All of us have done bad things in our lives, that's why we need the forgiveness of God. Your love one is no different. Think of the good things your love one has done, and you will find happiness in remembering those moments.

> Finally, brethren, whatsoever things are true, whatsoever things are honest, whatsoever things are just, whatsoever things are pure, whatsoever things are lovely, whatsoever things are good report. If there be any praise, think on these things. (Phil. 4:8)

If you spend most of your time watching and listening to bad news, how do you think you would feel? The Bible says the gospel is the good news, so if you would spend that same time reading your Bible, your day would be full of joy and happiness. Why do some people enjoy looking for the bad in people and never looking for the good? Take the memories of the bad and the good from your love one and find happiness in remembering them.

> O Lord, I have heard thy speech, and was afraid: O Lord revive thy work in the midst of the years, in the midst of the years make known in wrath remember mercy. (Hab. 3:2)

I believe remembering your love one can bring health to your body because it can take a lot of stress and tension off your mind. God never intended for us to worry or to be afraid about anything, but all of that changed when Satan trick Adam and Eve. If you would start to remember one thing daily, good or bad about your love one, you would start to heal quickly. I'm sure you have many memories good or bad about your love one, so start remembering.

Yeah though I walk through the valley of the shadow of death, I will fear no evil: for thou art with me: thy rod and thy staff they comfort me. (Ps. 23:4)

Remembering without ceasing your work of faith, and labor of love and patience of hope in our Lord Jesus Christ, in the sight of God and our faith. (1st Thess. 1:3)

When my eighteen-month-old daughter, Candice, was sick, I can remember praying to God until I cried for him to heal her, but she died. I was hurt and very sad, but I never blamed God. I knew Candice was okay because she was in his arms. So many people would blame God if that had happened to them, but what they don't understand is that God had a better plan for Candice. He would never do anything to bring you or your love one any harm. God is good and always will be. Remain faithful to him no matter what the situation is.

> He shall cover thee with his feathers, and under his wings shalt thou trust: his truth shall be thy shield and buckler. (Ps. 91:4)

One of the things I like to remember about my daughter, Candice, is when she would crawl on the floor and reach her arms out to me. She wanted me to pick her up and set her on my lap. You might think this would make me feel sad, but it actually it makes me feel good because it brings back the happy memories of that moment. God knows what we need to remember and forget. There is no way I could have gotten over the death of Candice without the help of God. He gave me the strength to do it.

> O Lord, my strength, and my fortress, and my refuge in the day of affliction, the gentiles shall come unto thee from the ends of the earth, and say

> surely our fathers have inherited lies, vanity, and things wherein there is no profit. (Jer. 16:19)

The only way you will find true peace when a love one dies is with the help of God. There will be some people that will tell you to stop thinking about them and move on with your life. That can be true in some cases because some people never get over the death of a love one. I believe it's okay to remember them, but don't let it stop you from having a normal life. You don't have to stop living because your love one died.

> Therefore being justified by faith, we have peace with God through our Lord Jesus Christ. (Rom. 5:1)

God wants you to have peace and understanding while remembering your love one. This can help heal some of the pain and sorrow you are going through. Never forget about them, but understand you can do nothing to bring them back. How many of you have lost something that was very precious to you? What's the first thing you did when you realize that it was lost? You try to remember the last place you had it. When you do find it, you are full of joy and happiness. That's the same way you will feel when you meet your love one again in heaven.

> These things have I spoken unto you, that my joy might remain in you, and that your joy might be full. (John 15:11)

When you have God in your life you can always be full of joy and happiness no matter what the situation is. Remembering your love ones shouldn't make you depressed, worried or unhappy. Lean on him, and he will show you how not to worry. Open your mind to the truth, and you will see that your love ones are in a better place, and one day you, will see them again.

> But Rejoice, in as much as you are partakers of Christ's suffering; that, when his glory

shall be revealed, ye may be
glad also with exceeding joy.
(1 Peter 4:13)

In those lonely times, when you are thinking of them, allow the joy and the peace of
God to be in your heart. This is where you will
gain your strength to overcome that lost.

# CHAPTER 5

**Peace**

**Webster's definition of peace—calm
and quiet state of accord, freedom from
troubling emotions or thoughts.**

There will come a time in everyone's life that you will need peace, especially during the time of the death of someone you love. The world we live in now it's very hard to find peace and love, so when we do find it, we need to cherish it. Everyone today seems to be on a fast pace course going nowhere, and those who don't know God only have time for themselves. God will never be like that. He always has time for everyone, and he is never troubled.

> Peace I leave with you, my peace I give unto you: not ass the world giveth, give I unto you, let not your heart be troubled, neither let it be afraid. (John 14:27)

You will never find true peace in this world because it's of Satan, and he offers those who follow him temporary fixes for their problems. The only way you will ever find true peace is through the love of God. Now I know during the time of the loss of your love one, it's really hard to find that peace because it's hard for you to trust anyone. When your emotions are out of control, you need to calm down and let the Holy Spirit help you.

> Who comforteh us in all our tribulation, that we may be able to comfort them which are in trouble, by the comfort wherewith we ourselves are comforted of God. (2 Cor. 1:4)

I know your family wants to comfort and help you, but it always seems not to be enough in times of bereavement. When they leave you alone, the pain seems to come back even stronger. Only God can comfort you and fill that emptiness and pain you are feeling. It is very hard to find comfort from anyone because you are too emotional. Even some of your closes friends in the church can't seem to help you. Most people are always in a hurry and want slow down for anyone including God, but he will always give you time and peace just have faith and trust in him.

> These things I have spoken unto you, that in me ye might have peace in the world ye shall have tribula-

tion: but be of good cheer:
I have overcome the world.
(John 16:33)

Satan will try to rob you of the blessings
that God gives you every day, including peace.
When you start to listen to him and believe
what he is saying, that's when your blessings
and peace will start to leave you.

Keep God in your heart during your time
of tragedy, and you will never lose the peace he
will give you. Man will never be able to provide
you with the peace you need during your time
of lost, only God can. There are not too many
people in this world that can provide you some
of the peace you need—maybe your pastor
and some of your family members, but most of
them will also need help in finding it. Always
remember to call on God first when you need
help, and he will give you what you need.

For Kings and for all that are
in authority; that we may
lead a quiet and peaceable life
in all godliness and honesty.
(Tim. 2:2)

Most people get very hysterical and emotional when someone they love dies. This is a normal reaction for anyone including Christians. God knew we would need him to give us peace and comfort during these times, and he would always be there to do it. There is no one that cares about your feelings more than God. He wants you to have rest and not to worry about anything. There can be some friends and family members in your life not really concerned about your feelings during your time of grief, but God will always be concerned for you.

> And came and preached peace
> to you which were afar off, and
> to them that were nigh. (Eph.
> 2:17)

God will never leave you alone in your time of trouble. He will always be there to help you get through it. But most of the time, we are not willing to let God do this, and we end up having so much distress, pain, sorrow and no peace. The Holy Spirit will speak to you and give you the inner peace you need to get over this lost, but Satan will try to rob you of it. Can you picture yourself early in the morning sitting on your back porch, drinking a cup of coffee and listening to the birds playing? Now, I would say that's a peaceful moment, wouldn't you? Always listen to God spirit and you will find what you need.

That kind of peace doesn't come along every day, but when it does, we need to give thanks to God for it. Satan always tries to disrupt the good things that he is giving us in our lives, but God won't allow him to. Can you imagine the peace the woman had when Jesus healed her of the sickness with the issue of blood she had for so many years? I know she couldn't stop thanking him and rejoicing; she could now finally have rest and peace she was so desperately searching for. The doctors or her family couldn't give her that. She only could receive that from Jesus.

Rejoice in the Lord always
again I say rejoice. (Phil. 4:4)

We as Christians have this to be very proud of. We serve a God that really cares about us. He wants us to be happy while we live here on this earth and receive eternal life when we die. I can remember when I was a young boy, lying in bed, listening to the rain hitting the tin roof on my dad's house. I could get some peace from that sound and found myself falling asleep just listening to it. Everyone in the house seemed to be asleep but me. I allowed the sound of the rain to give me peace in my mind and rest. God gives us that same type of peace when we allow him to.

> And I will pray the father, and he shall give you another comforter, that he may abide with you forever. (John 14:16)

The Holy Spirit will never leave you if you accept him. He knows you need comfort and peace while living here on this earth and no one can give you that but him.

Even the spirit of truth; whom the world cannot receive, because it seeth him not, neither knoweth him: but ye know him for he dwelleth with you, and shall be in you. (John 14:17)

Unfortunately, we live in a world of tragedy and grief that has no boundaries, and we see it everywhere. But here's the good news, no matter what comes our way, we can overcome it with the help of God. Trust in him with all your heart and your grief won't remain because he won't let it. He will provide you the strength you need to overcome it.

Then he said unto them, go your way, eat the fat, and drink the sweet, and send portions unto them for whom nothing is prepared: for this day is holy unto our Lord: neither be ye sorry; for the joy of the Lord is your strength. (Neh. 8:10)

The death of a love one is very hard to get over, and sometimes you feel like your life will never be the same again. Satan is a deceiver and a liar, he would have you to believe that, but God has defeated Satan in all his lies. God created life. The Bible teaches that God created all things for good. Death was never meant to be good, but it does exist because of sin. There is not a family in this world that hasn't faced this tragedy or had to endure the pain it brings. Thank God for all the peace he gives us during these times because everyone will need it.

> Blessed are they that mourn;
> for they shall be comforted.
> (Matt. 5:4)

God knew we would need someone to comfort us when we are going through difficult times. This should bring you some peace, knowing he really cares about you. We all can receive peace from God when we need it. Satan would like death to have the final say, but thanks to God that will never happen. If you are truly searching for peace during your time of bereavement, just continue to pray to God, and he will give it to you. It is hard for us as humans to find peace and understanding when a love one dies, but God can show us how.

I know I would have not found peace without the help of God when my daughter, Candice, died. God brought comfort to my heart and showed me she was okay, and everything would be all right. I know it's hard to find peace when you lose someone close to you; but in time, with the love of God, your pain will heal, and you will find peace and understanding.

Remember, God will never forsake you during your time of grief, and we all one day will have to face this moment in our lives, but thanks be to God we don't have to face it alone.

For me to live in Christ, and
to die is gain. (Phil. 1:21)

# CHAPTER 6

# Love for a Sister

### Webster's definition of love—warm concern, powerful attraction to another

> Beloved, let us love one
> another: for love is of God;
> and every one that loveth is
> born of God, and knoweth
> God. (John 4:7)

L ove is a powerful and wonderful thing that we all have expressed about someone we really care about. But when one of your siblings dies, it's a totally different kind of love we express for them. I grew up in and family of ten brothers and sisters where we all love each other very much. Dorothy, Terry, Martha Ann, Joann, Kathy, and I were the first six of the ten siblings. We did everything together, including sleeping in the same beds. When we played games, Joann was always my partner; and when me and my brother, Terry, needed our hair braided, she would always do mine. You might be thinking that she was my favorite sister, no, that's not the case, we never had any favorites in my family—we all are very close.

Joann may not have been the smartest in her books, but what she lacked in book knowledge, she made up for it in heart. She always had a good heart and a quiet spirit. You couldn't help but love her, she was so innocent. She always tried to do everything right, including her schoolwork, but it wasn't easy for her. When my mom passed, my dad relied on Joann to do the cooking because my sister, Dorothy, was in college. I enjoyed eating a lot of hamburger helper because that's what she mostly cooked, and I enjoyed eating moon pies too, which was her favorite sweet. I had so much fun growing up with Joann and my other brothers and sisters. When you come from a large family, there are no lonely times, but you might need some private time.

There were always games we made up and someone to play them with. We were almost never bored. Our parents raised us to play together and love each other, and that's what we did. You will never be a happy family together unless you love each other—this is what God intended for us. We played one game that we called playhouse—me and my brother, Terry, helped our sisters make small play areas that they called there playhouse. We would visit each one of their playhouses when they played in them. It was a good time, and we had so much fun being together. As we grew older, we started thinking about getting married.

Joann had never really dated before until she met Ronnie, who later became her husband. They married and had several children. Later on, after all the children became adults, she got sick. They took her to the doctor, and they diagnosed her with lymphoma; she died about two years later. When Joann died, I felt emptiness and a loss in my heart that I'm still getting over today. I will never forget her, and I still visit her grave often. God has taken Joann on to heaven to be with him, and he showed me that she's in a much better place now. Death can come unexpectedly, so love your family, your neighbors, and your friends while they are alive. Remember, death is not the end, it's a new beginning.

So when this corruptible shall have put on incorruptible, and this mortal shall have put on immortality, then shall be brought to pass the saying that is written, death is swallowed up in victory. O death, where is thy sting? O grave, where is thy victory? (1 Cor. 15:54–55)

# EPILOGUE

I got the inspiration to write this book from a lady that was my customer. She came in one day with her husband, looking to buy a travel trailer. I showed them some on the lot, and when we returned back inside and sit at the tables, she began to cry. I asked what was wrong, and she said she couldn't buy a camper from me because her father had died. I told her not to worry about buying a camper, and if she didn't mind, I would start sending her some scriptures that would help her. I started sending her scriptures that would help her cope with the death of her father. Later on, God gave me this book idea, *Comfort in Time of Bereavement*, to help comfort everyone who will and has lost a love one.

Looking back on writing this book, it has really given me peace of mind to understand when my sister Joann died December 28,

2017, that she was Ok, and I would see her again. I found comfort in knowing that she was a woman of God, and genuinely believed in him. So, I know without a doubt, she is resting in the arms of Jesus in heaven.

# ABOUT THE AUTHOR

Gerome Singleterry was born in Jemison, Alabama, in 1953. His parents are Walter and Myrtle Singleterry. He graduated from Jemison High School in 1971, became a Christian at an early age, and now attend King Wood Church in Alabaster Alabama. He is born-again and truly loves God with all his heart. He is happily married to Donna, and they have three daughters—Gabrielle, Stephanie, and Tracy. They also have two grandchildren, Destin and Kayla. He got the idea to write this book from one of his customers.